THE ROYAL MINT
An Illustrated History

G.P. Dyer
Librarian and Curator, Royal Mint

CONTENTS

Front cover.
'The Queen's Shilling,' a late nineteenth-century painting by the Hon. John Collier.

FOREWORD

1986 is a year of celebration for the Royal Mint. Exactly 1100 years ago, in 886AD, Alfred the Great occupied London and there followed a large issue of silver pennies bearing his portrait and the name LONDONIA in the form of a monogram.

The striking of coins in London was not new, and indeed a mint had been briefly established there by the Romans. But from Alfred's time minting in London was more or less continuous, and as the following pages show there is a thread which links the modern Royal Mint to those far-off events.

This year therefore provides a happy opportunity to reflect on the long history of the Royal Mint: on its development from the workshops of the Anglo-Saxon moneyers, to a single mint within the walls of the Tower of London, onto custom-built premises at Tower Hill, and finally to the new mint at Llantrisant in South Wales.

A commemorative medal is being struck and public exhibitions are being arranged at Goldsmiths' Hall in London and at the National Museum of Wales in Cardiff. This booklet is another part of these celebrations and I hope that it, too, will help to convey a sense of the pride felt by myself and my colleagues at the Royal Mint.

Jeremy Gerhard

D.J. Gerhard, CB
Deputy Master and Comptroller

Medal struck by the Royal Mint in 1986 to commemorate 1100 years in minting.

ORIGINS

Above. Celtic gold stater.

Early Minting in London

Minting began in Britain in the first century BC. The earliest coins, crude imitations of coins of Marseilles, were cast in moulds; but soon, though still imitations of Continental types, coins were being struck by hand in much the same way as they were to be made for the next 1500 years.

The coinage of the Celtic tribes ceased with the Roman conquest. Thereafter Roman coins, the universal currency in the Western Empire, circulated in Britain, and for a time from the end of the third century AD Roman coins were actually struck at a mint in London. This London mint set up by the Romans is the earliest recorded mint in the capital, and its coins may be recognised by the presence of a mintmark, of which PLN is one of the best known versions. Established by the usurper Carausius (287-293), it became an official mint after the defeat of the rebellion and its substantial output of bronze coin continued until 325AD, when it was closed by the Emperor Constantine the Great. It enjoyed a brief revival in the year 383AD, when it was re-opened by another usurping Emperor, Magnus Maximus (383-388), but is believed to have closed again almost at once.

Above. Billon *'follis'* of Constantine the Great, struck in London.

Right. The mintmark PLN (enlarged).

Following the withdrawal of the Romans early in the fifth century no coins seem to have been struck in Britain for perhaps some 200 years. Native gold coins began to appear about 630AD and within fifty years or so gold had been entirely superseded by silver. These silver coins, known as sceattas, are the first English pennies and were inspired by the deniers or denarii of the Merovingian Franks. And it was again in imitation of the Franks that from the middle of the eighth century a silver penny was introduced of similar weight but of larger diameter. In the North, however, very debased sceattas or stycas continued to be issued until the middle of the ninth century.

London moneyers were in operation from soon after 650 AD. Since the coins do not normally bear any specific indication of where they were struck, the scale and duration of minting activity in London during the next two centuries is somewhat uncertain. Towards the end of the eighth century coins began regularly to carry the names of the kings for whom they were struck and of the moneyers who produced them; and scholars have identified a series of coins as belonging to London, that 'most renowned place and

Above. Silver penny of Coenwulf, King of Mercia (796-821).

Above. London penny of Egbert, King of Wessex.

royal town'. The London coins are usually in the names of Mercian kings, and the most extensive issues are by Coenwulf (796-821) and Burgred (852-874). But remarkably enough an extremely rare penny of Egbert of Wessex (802-839), struck during a brief period when he ruled all Southern England, is the only one that proves its London origin by bearing on the reverse the inscription LVNDONIA CIVIT.

Although the output of London moneyers was substantial at the end of Burgred's reign, London was customarily a less important mint than Canterbury, and its production was on more than one occasion disrupted by the attacks of the Danes.

Growing Pre-eminence of London

In 886AD Alfred the Great (871-899) occupied London, and according to the Anglo-Saxon Chronicle 'all the English people that were not under subjection to the Danes submitted to him.' A large issue of silver pennies soon followed this success, showing on the obverse a stylised portrait of the king and on the reverse the

Right. Athelstan's mints. The location of four mints is not certain and they have therefore been excluded.

Above. Monogram penny of Alfred the Great.

name LONDONIA in the form of a monogram. In a real sense this spectacular issue marks a notable milestone in the history of minting in London, for from this time control of minting in London passed permanently out of Mercian hands into the hands of the West Saxon kings from whom our present royal family is descended.

During the reign of Alfred's grandson Athelstan (924-939), who styled himself 'King of the Whole of Britain,' an attempt was made to secure a uniform coinage. At the Council of Grateley about 928 AD monetary laws were promulgated which ordained that 'there is to be one coinage over all the king's dominion, and no one is to mint money except in a town.' The laws form the earliest surviving legislation relating to coinage and by specifying that eight moneyers should operate in London the Grateley decrees are also the first to regulate minting in London. Though at least fifteen moneyers, among them Beahred, Biorneard, Grimwald and Liofhelm, are now known to have struck coins of Athelstan in London, this number need not be inconsistent with the prescribed quota if a substantial turnover of moneyers is assumed.

Above. The Grateley decrees. A manuscript fragment in the British Library.

The great reform of Edgar (959-975) authorised coins of new type to circulate throughout England. The reverse incorporated the name of the mint as well as that of the moneyer, enabling several new mints to be identified and indicating that their number now stood at perhaps three dozen or so. By the reign of Ethelred II (978-1016) coins were being struck in more than seventy different towns, mostly to be found in the southern half of the country. Such a large number of mints may seem surprising to those familiar with the modern monopoly of the Royal Mint, but at that time communications were not easy and it was not practical for merchants to be too far from a mint. In any case mints were not then the large scale factories that they have now become and it may be helpful to think of them more as blacksmith's shops. Undoubtedly they were small establishments, presided over by an authorised number of moneyers licensed to receive dies, and functioning intermittently only as and when their services were required by merchants. Possibly even in London the eight moneyers authorised by Athelstan operated in separate shops rather than as a single unit.

Above. Penny of Athelstan, struck in London by the moneyer Biorneard.

The simple process of coining began with silver bullion being melted in small crucibles. Poured onto a slab to cool, the silver was beaten to a thin plate from which blanks were cut with shears and struck by hand between a pair of dies. The pile, or lower die, had a spiked end to enable it to be driven firmly into a block of wood; a blank was placed on top of the pile and above it was held the trussel or upper die. The trussel then received blows from a hammer, causing the blank to be impressed with the obverse and reverse designs.

Dies were produced on average at the rate of two trussels to one pile, for the trussel by sustaining the direct blows of the

hammer was subjected to greater wear and tear. It was therefore the custom for the trussel to bear the reverse design, since this was simpler and more easy to replace than the royal portrait which by now normally appeared on the obverse. Yet even the portrait may not have been that difficult to reproduce, being constructed by small chisel-like punches showing crescents, pellets, wedges and bars.

Above. Britannia striking coins by hand. Detail from a Royal Mint souvenir medal of 1924.

Right. Seal of William I, 1066 - 1087. (Actual size 84mm)

Above. London penny of William I.

Below. Silver penny of Henry I, struck in London by the moneyer Dereman.

By the time of the Norman Conquest the number of mints had begun to decline. The Conquest itself left the coinage surprisingly undisturbed and indeed it seems that the vast majority of moneyers were confirmed in office. The name Deorman, for instance, continues to appear on the coins of London, and the family of that Deorman who is mentioned in the Domesday Book can be linked with minting in London through perhaps four or five generations. It was a family prominent in the life of the city, for one of its members was a canon of St Paul's, another looks to have been an alderman, and a third was a justiciar under Stephen (1135-1154). Their high social status and the performance of important civic duties imply that their minting responsibilities would need to be delegated, probably to other, more active moneyers.

In this Norman period, about ten moneyers were perhaps active at any one time in London. They appear to have continued to operate independently at first, though in view of the strong family associations it may be that not all the moneyers had separate establishments. The most likely area where they worked is around St Paul's, where goldsmiths congregated, but it is possible that there were also minting workshops near the Walbrook and close to modern Lombard Street. What is at least clear is that as the number of mints outside the capital declined after the Conquest so the pre-eminence of the London mint became more firmly established.

THE TOWER MINT

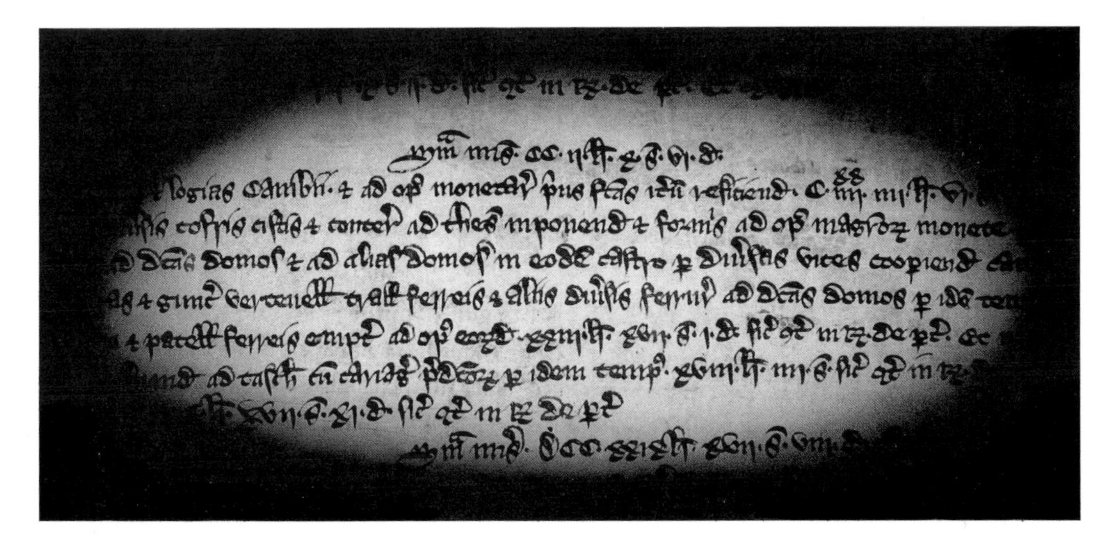

Above. Extract from the Pipe Roll for 1280 - 1281, recording expenditure on buildings for the Mint in the Tower.

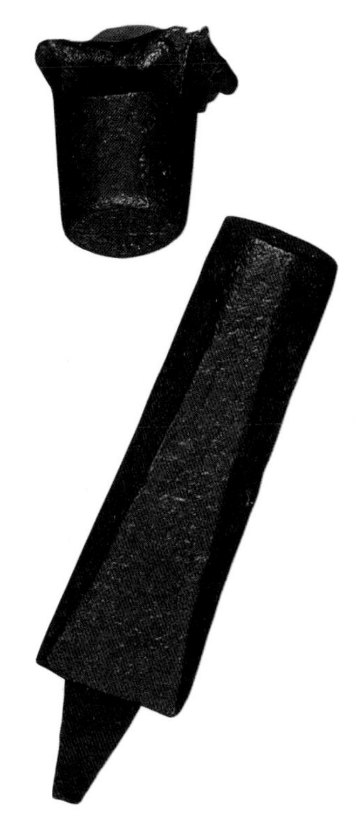

Above. Medieval pile and trussel. Used in the mint at York for the striking of half-groats, c. 1353 - 1355.

The Move to the Tower

During the second half of the twelfth century the work of the individual London moneyers becomes rather more closely linked, suggesting that they were at last housed in a single location. In the thirteenth century this mint is placed by one account in Old Change, conveniently close to the goldsmiths' quarter in Cheapside. Other writers have suggested that by 1248 the mint may already have been in the Tower of London, and certainly by about 1279 it enjoyed the safety of secure quarters within the Tower. Between the years 1279 and 1281 the Pipe Roll records the expenditure of £729.17s.8½d for work on the Mint in the Tower, and there are references to the purchase of timber for Mint houses and lodges, to tiling, thatching and plastering, and to the provision, among other things, of coffers, chests and containers in which to put treasure and dies. But there is no real indication of its precise position within the Tower, and it is not altogether certain if the Mint's first quarters in the Tower were in the area which it subsequently occupied between the inner and outer walls.

At the same time the subordination of the other mints to London was confirmed by the appointment in 1279 of William de Turnemire as master moneyer throughout England. Turnemire came from Marseilles and, bringing with him new processes for coining money, provides an early illustration of a strong and continuing French influence on the development of minting processes in England. The metal was now cast in sand moulds into long bars, of smaller cross section than the surface area of the coin; blanks were cut from these bars with a chisel and then, with the help of several annealings, were hammered flat and rounded before being struck between a pair of dies in the accustomed manner.

The coinage, too, was developing. For 500 years it had consisted almost entirely of silver pennies, the need for small

Above. Cut halfpenny and farthing.

Right. Gold noble of Edward III (Actual size 33.5mm)

change being satisfied by cutting the penny into halves and quarters in order to produce halfpennies and farthings. Now from 1279/80, round halfpennies and farthings were struck, and the range of denominations was further increased by a large silver groat or fourpence, clearly inspired by the French gros tournois. An attempt in the 1250s to introduce a gold penny had failed, but from the 1340s gold was also to become a regular feature of Mint output with the striking of gold nobles and, much later, of angels.

Above. New silver farthing, halfpenny and groat of Edward I.

Mint organisation was adopting a more formal structure. The 'keeper of the changes, workmen, coiners and ministers and other officers' of the mints in London and elsewhere in the country were incorporated by Edward I (1272-1307). The charter was confirmed by Edward II, and in due course by Edward III, Richard II and the Lancastrian kings. These early charters gave the Mint officers certain freedoms, including exemption from various forms of taxation and from public obligations such as service on juries. They are therefore generally concerned with the grant of personal privileges and immunities to those employed on this particular branch of the king's service. As regards the actual duties and management of the king's mints, these from the time of Turnemire came to be governed by an indenture or contract between the king and the Master of the Mint. This grew into an extensive code, prescribing the weights and fineness of the various coins, the rates of seigniorage, the coinage charges, and the duties of the principal officers. The Master was accordingly a contractor of the crown, receiving his remuneration by prescribed charges, out of which he had to provide tools, defray waste, pay his journeymen, and make a profit.

None was trusted and the system incorporated a number of safeguards. The Master had to provide security, two or more independent officers had to concur in every action, and the Warden was present as the immediate representative of the king. Supervision of weight and fineness was essential, since a dishonest Master had the opportunity to debase the coinage and make extra profit.

Right. Gold angel of Edward IV (Actual size 26.5mm)

Below. Gold and silver trial plates of 1477, against which sample coins were checked at the Trial of the Pyx.

The exchequer, whose concern for such matters requires no explanation, had long since instituted its own check on the accuracy of the coinage. This developed into the Trial of the Pyx, where sample coins were tested by an independent jury, and the earliest surviving writ calling for such a trial about 1282 already speaks of it as a well established procedure. Nor was it a formality. In 1318 silver coins were found to be below standard, while in 1349 it was the gold coinage which was found to be deficient. For the first of these misdemeanours the Master of the Mint was imprisoned and, for the second, fined.

Consolidation in the Tower

By the middle of the fourteenth century the whole of the coinage was more or less concentrated in the Tower of London, though other mints still functioned from time to time. The few remaining ecclesiastical mints ceased during the reign of Henry VIII, so that from then on, except in times of emergency such as during the great debasement (1544-1551) or the silver recoinage (1696-1698), the Mint in the Tower was normally the only mint in operation.

The Mint buildings are known in the fifteenth century to have occupied the narrow space between the inner and outer walls, extending perhaps as far as Legge's Mount by the end of the century and by the beginning of Elizabeth I's reign stretching all the way round to the Salt Tower. Extensive alterations had accompanied Wolsey's reform of the currency in 1526, involving the erection of a new gold shearing house and a receipt house. The latter sounds particularly grand, being adorned with the Royal Arms and Badges, stone chimney pieces, twenty-two feet of Burgundy glass, and eighty-eight feet of Normandy glass. Further building work was undertaken in 1566, and again in 1585/86 when a timber-framed office was erected with a 'grete duble chimney' and a 'great Baye window.' The elongated horse-shoe arrangement of the Mint was confirmed, with the various processes apparently spread out somewhat inconveniently among several different houses and rooms.

Foreign influence in the management of the Mint became less strong and senior appointments were increasingly made from among the goldsmiths in the City of London. Not infrequently politics played a part and sometimes dangerously so, for Mint officers were among those who perished at Tewkesbury and Bosworth. Lord Hastings, another Mint officer, lost his head for opposing Richard III.

A Mint Board, consisting of the three principal posts of Warden, Master and Comptroller, emerged under Edward IV and that same king confirmed and extended the privileges of Mint officers in a Royal Charter of 20 February 1462. The new charter incorporated the officers into 'one bodie perpetuall and one

Below. Plan of the Tower of London by Hayward and Gascoigne, 1597.

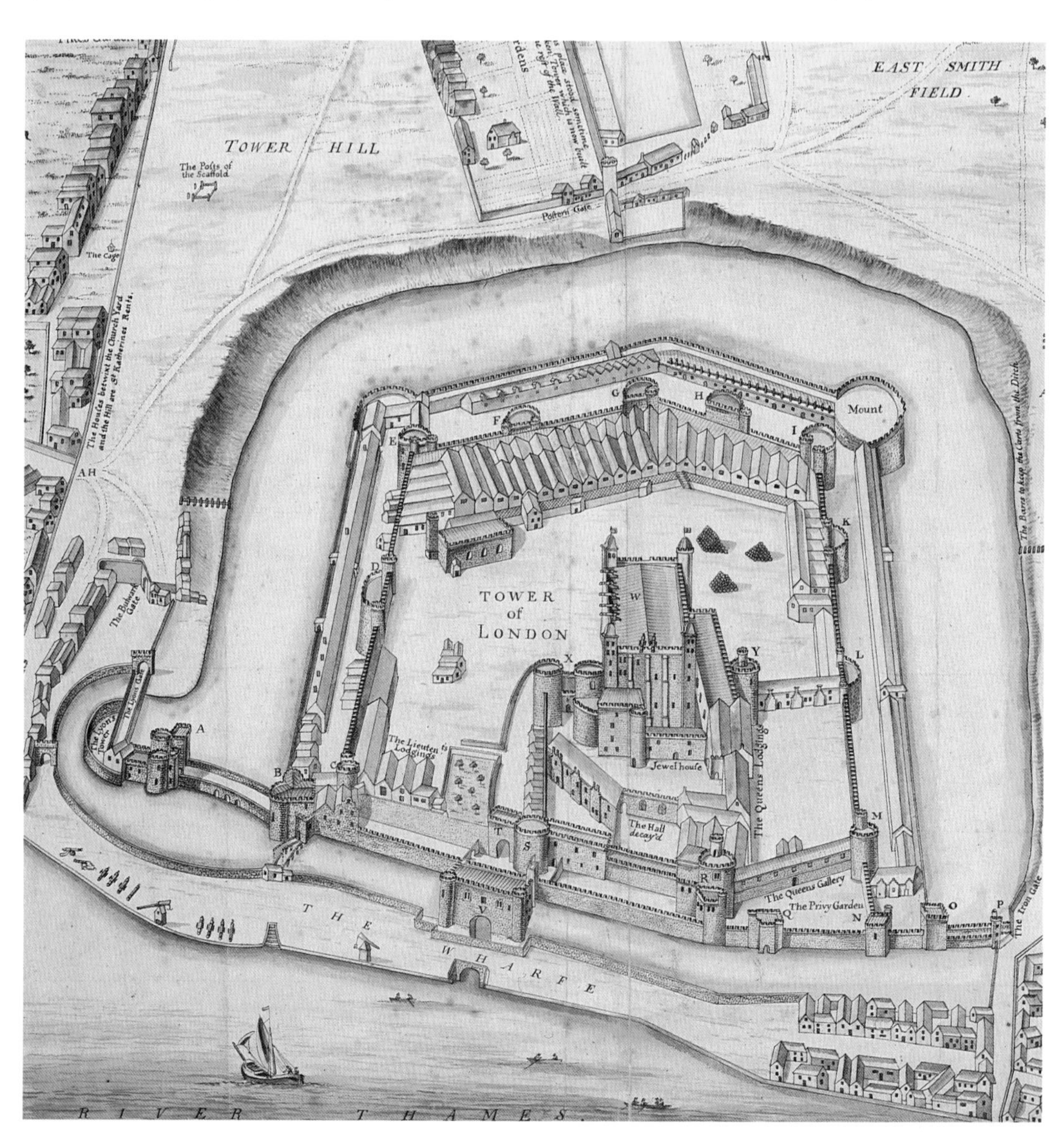

Above. The new shilling or testoon, with its realistic portrait of Henry VII (1485 - 1509).

Below. Enthroned portrait of Henry VII on the new gold sovereign.

commonaltie perpetualle', with the right amongst other things to own land and to take legal proceedings. This improved status was said by the new charter to be in response to their representations that 'they and ther predycessors ... for the doubte ambyguite darcknes and dyffycultis of certen generall wordes and termes ... haue bynne molestead Inquyeted and vexed.' From this inconvenience, according to the charter, they were entitled to protection since mint work was a subsidiary and occasional employment which drew men from 'ther owne propre busynez' and which could indeed see them assigned to a distant place like Canterbury or Calais. The enlarged charter was confirmed in turn by Henry VII, Henry VIII, Edward VI and Mary I, and on 26 November 1559 by Elizabeth I.

Right. Silver crown of Edward VI, 1552.

Below. Debased shilling or testoon of Henry VIII (1509 - 1547).

The coinage itself began to take on a modern appearance. Until the closing years of the reign of Henry VII a stylised representation of the monarch had been deemed sufficient for the obverse of the coinage but now an attempt was made to achieve a recognisable portrait. Reverse designs, too, had become more adventurous, with heraldry providing an aesthetically more pleasing alternative to the familiar cross. In the range of denominations the coinage had also advanced. A gold sovereign of twenty shillings had appeared in 1489, a silver shilling followed a few years later, and in 1551 the new silver coinage of crown, halfcrown, shilling, sixpence, threepence, penny and halfpenny has a decidedly modern ring to it.

The 1551 issue in fact represented a restoration of the coinage. Since 1542, in a misguided attempt to raise money, it had been progressively debased by Henry VIII and his successor. Some £4,000,000 of this inferior coin had been produced and though no more was struck after 1551 much of it was still in circulation when Elizabeth I came to the throne in 1558. A complete recoinage was long overdue and this was at last undertaken in 1560 and 1561 with the help of an additional but temporary mint in the Tower of London alongside the existing mint. For the Queen the laying to

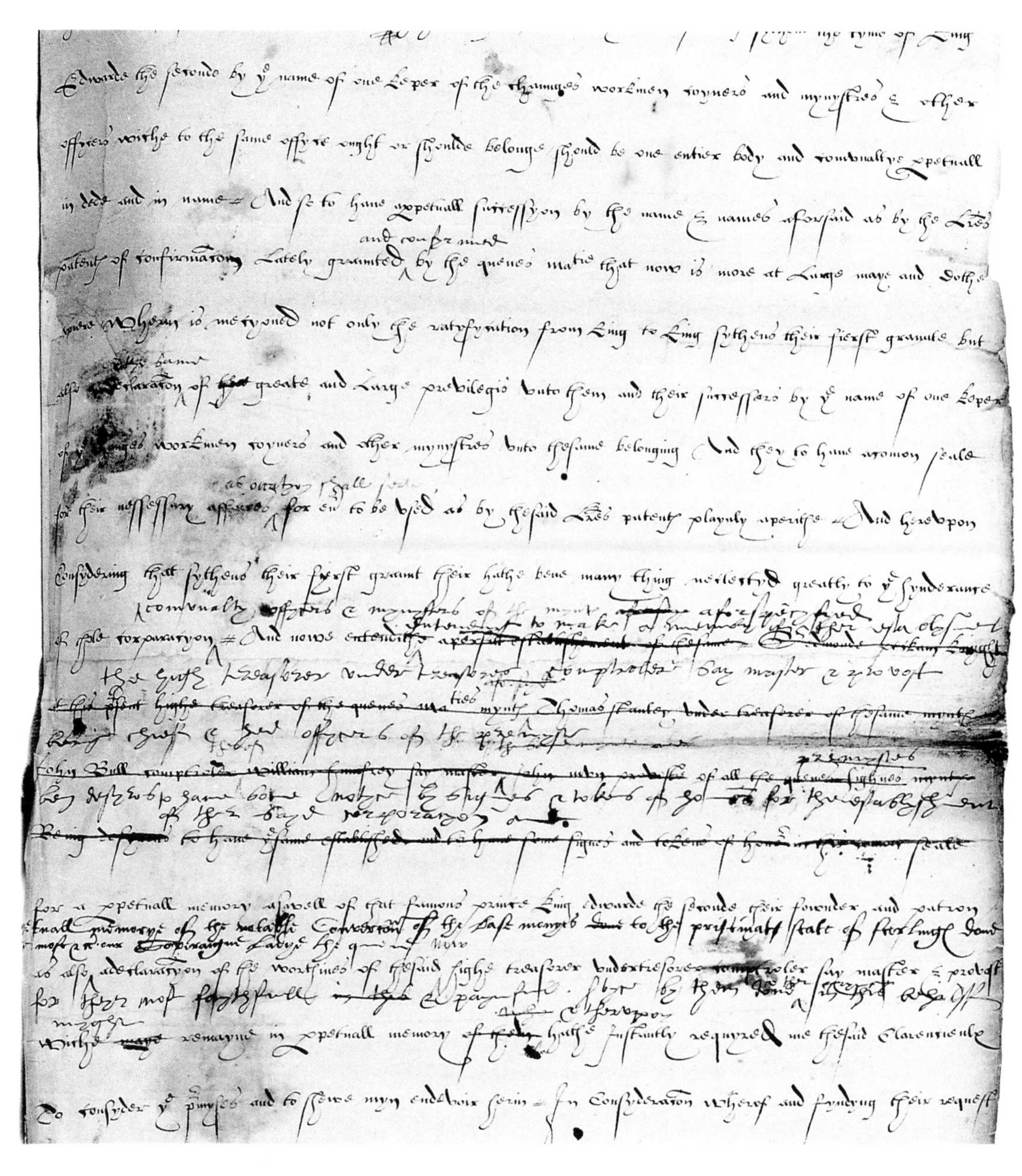

Above. Draft Grant of Arms to the Mint Corporation, 1561-2.

rest of the 'hideous monster of the base moneys' came to be recognised as one of her greatest achievements, and it may be taken as a sign of her personal satisfaction that she visited the mints in the Tower on 10 July 1561.

Her satisfaction was matched by that of the Mint officers, whose success in the 'notable convercion of the base monyes to the pristinat state of sterlings' prompted them to seek the privilege of Arms for the Mint Corporation. The Arms subsequently drawn up by Clarenceux King of Arms are dominated by the personal devices

of the five leading officers, apparently arranged in order of seniority: first, the cross-crosslets of Sir Edmund Pekham, the high treasurer; next, the stag's or hart's heads of Thomas Stanley, the under treasurer; then the bull's heads of John Bull, the comptroller, and the fleur-de-lis of William Humfrey, the assay master; and finally the castles of John Monnes, the Provost of the Company of Moneyers. Whether the Arms were ever used, however, is open to doubt.

Above. Contemporary medallic portraits of Thomas Stanley and Sir Richard Martin. (Actual size 44mm and 58 mm respectively)

Right. The Coat of Arms of the Mint Corporation, blazoned by Clarenceux King of Arms in 1561/2.

Below. Gold trial plate of 1542. The little bow in the bottom corner is probably an allusion to Sir Martin Bowes.

That Thomas Stanley was a goldsmith is a reminder of the importance to the Mint both of individual goldsmiths and of their Company. Stanley, for instance, had been in charge of the main Tower mint during the recoinage and remained in control until his death in 1571. A little earlier in the century, the Mint had been dominated by Sir Martin Bowes (1496-1566), Prime Warden of the Goldsmiths' Company and Lord Mayor of London. Later another prominent goldsmith, Sir Richard Martin (1534-1617), controlled the fortunes of the Mint for an extended period of some forty-five years. Goldsmiths, too, served on the jury at the Trial of the Pyx and their skills were also utilised in the making of the trial plates against which the fineness of the coins was checked.

For the moment minting processes remained largely unchanged, though the sheer size of the crown pieces struck from

Above. Milled shilling of Elizabeth I, struck by Eloy Mestrell.

Right. Minting in the Tower in the reign of Elizabeth I.

Below. Portcullis Money. Struck in the Tower and shipped to the East Indies in 1601, the coins were one of the first export orders undertaken by the Mint.

Below. Sir William Parkhurst, Warden of the Mint at the beginning of the Civil War. (Actual size 76.5mm)

1551 perhaps speaks for some form of mechanical assistance. Mechanisation had been taken much further on the Continent, particularly in France, but at home it was resisted by the moneyers, who operated as a private company under contract to the Master. Led by a provost, they were responsible for the actual operations of coining and over the centuries they had turned themselves into an intensely private and self-perpetuating body which jealously guarded its rights and privileges and which, like a medieval guild, kept its secrets to itself. The attempt by the Frenchman Eloy Mestrell to introduce machinery in the 1560s was accordingly a failure, despite the undoubted superiority of his milled coins. Poor Mestrell, frustrated and unhappy, took up counterfeiting and was duly hanged.

Mechanisation

During the Civil War, though it continued to strike coins with the name and portrait of Charles I, the Tower Mint was in the hands of the Parliamentarians, obliging the King to provide for himself in a series of temporary mints in Exeter, Oxford, Shrewsbury, York and elsewhere. Certain of the Mint officers at the Tower, among them Sir William Parkhurst the Warden, left to support the King. A few, like Nicholas Briot, endeavoured to serve both sides but most remained at their posts. Nevertheless, with the establishment of the Commonwealth in 1649, there was a considerable turnover of senior personnel as loyal Parliamentarians such as

Above. Machine-struck crowns of Charles I and Oliver Cromwell.

Above Right. Thomas Simon's design for one side of the Commonwealth Seal 1651. (Actual size 145mm)

Below. Commonwealth halfcrown of 1651, struck by the old methods.

Dr Aaron Guerdain, Thomas Barnardiston and Samuel Bartlett were rewarded by high office in the Mint.

Briot, a skilful Frenchman, had been allowed under Charles I to strike coins in a press. If in the end he enjoyed as little success as Mestrell, at least the claims of those who supported mechanisation were becoming more difficult to refute. Interest continued during the Commonwealth and the moneyers put up their own man, David Ramage, to demonstrate that they, too, could strike coins by machine. It was another Frenchman, however, Peter Blondeau, who showed with his splendid portrait coins of Cromwell what could really be achieved by the new processes. Finally the restored Charles II, perhaps shamed by the unfortunate contrast between his coins and those of Louis XIV, authorised Blondeau to install machinery in the Mint and to 'direct and Instruct the Monyers in Coyning the Gold and Silver Moneys by way of ye Mill and press...' This he did, at a cost of £2,710 for the machinery and its installation.

Under the new system the molten metal was ladled into moulds of sand, producing cast fillets of the breadth and little more than the thickness of the intended coin. These fillets were reduced by a rolling mill, operated by horses tramping round a cellar below, and from the fillets blanks were punched by a small fly press. The striking of the blanks was performed in a simple and effective screw press, which brought down the upper die onto the blank by the action of a large screw carrying the die in a holder mounted at its

Above. Medallic portrait, believed to be of the Mint engraver Thomas Simon. (Actual size 28mm across)

Right. Simon's famous Petition Crown of 1663. The edge contains in tiny letters his petition to the King for his work to be used instead of that of a rival engraver. (Actual size 40mm)

Below. Milled coins of Charles II. A guinea of 1663 and, *below,* one of the new copper halfpennies first issued along with copper farthings in 1672.

Above. Medal of Thomas Neale Master of the Mint 1686-1699.

lower end. The screw was set in motion by workmen pulling at the weighted ends of a long horizontal bar and descended with great force to hit the blank resting on the bottom die. Blanks could be struck at the rate of one every two seconds, but it was extremely tiring and the teams of workmen could not work for long at a time. Even less to be envied was the moneyer, who had the task of flicking the newly- struck coin away from the dies and putting a fresh blank in its place. Yet legend has it that the most skilled moneyers found it possible to feed a press and read a newspaper at the same time.

On one point Blondeau insisted on secrecy. This concerned the method of rounding the blanks and rolling on the graining or lettering which distinguished the edges of the new coins. Those responsible for this part of the process were obliged to swear on oath that they would not disclose how it was done. The oath survived Blondeau's death and continued to be administered for the next 150 years, until long after details of the process had been revealed on the Continent.

According to the diarist Samuel Pepys, an occasional visitor to the Tower, the transformed Mint could strike up to £24,000 a week. Though more expensive to produce, the milled coins were far superior to the old hammered pieces, being rounder, thicker and better struck; and with their grained or lettered edges they were also much more difficult to clip and to counterfeit. Production began in 1662 and regular use of the hammer was abandoned the following year. The Commonwealth coins, which understandably offended delicate political susceptibilities, were quickly withdrawn and replaced, but it was not until the end of the century that the remaining hammered silver coins were called in. The huge recoinage of 1696-1698 was more than the Tower Mint could cope with unaided, and branch mints were temporarily established at Bristol, Chester, Exeter, Norwich and York.

At the Tower coining capacity was increased and scores of extra workmen were recruited. New buildings were erected under the supervision of Sir Christopher Wren and additional rolling mills, blank- cutting machines and coining presses were installed. By these means an unprecedented amount of £5,000,000 in silver coin was produced by the Tower Mint between 1696 and 1698.

Below right. Copy retained by Newton of an official submission to the Lords Commissioners of the Treasury, 1715.

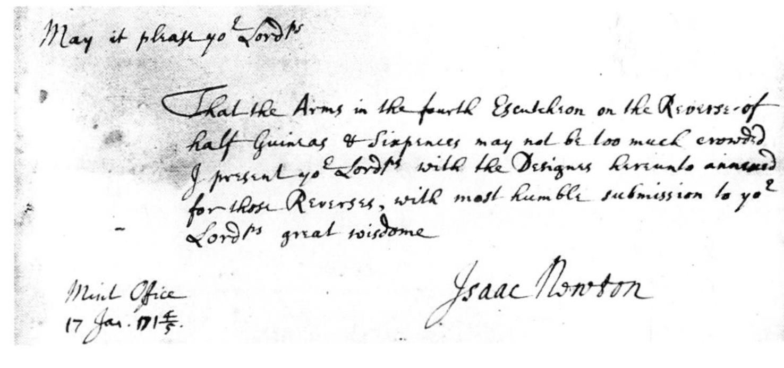

May it please yo.r Lord.ps

That the Arms in the fourth Escutcheon on the Reverse of half Guineas & Sixpences may not be too much crowded I present yo.r Lord.ps with the Designes hereunto annexed for those Reverses, with most humble submission to yo.r Lord.ps great wisdome

Mint Office
17 Jan. 171 4/5.

Isaac Newton

Above. Medallic portrait of Newton by John Croker, Chief Engraver of the Mint from 1705 to 1741. (Actual size 51.5mm)

Sir Isaac Newton

The recoinage coincided with the arrival at the Tower of the most famous Mint officer of all time, Sir Isaac Newton. He had been appointed Warden in 1696, but it had not been intended that the great scientist should devote himself to the Mint, and the Chancellor of the Exchequer had been quick to tell him that the post 'has not too much bus'ness to require more attendance than you may spare.'

Yet from the start he chose to throw himself into the work, becoming fully involved in the apprehension and prosecution of counterfeiters. The twilight world of informers and criminals was perhaps distasteful to Newton but that 'old dogg, the Warden' proved a doughty opponent and saw even the extraordinary rogue William Chaloner to the gallows. In 1699 he became Master of the Mint, a technically less senior but financially more rewarding post than that of Warden, and he remained Master until his death on 20 March 1727 at the age of eighty-four. There is evidence of a continuing involvement in the surviving volumes of his Mint papers, full of carefully revised drafts in his own cramped hand. It is clear that a mind capable of giant leaps of imagination was also at home with the activities of the Mint and followed them through in minutest detail. Only as he became weakened by age and infirmity did his grip slacken on the daily round of Mint affairs.

Above. Walnut cabinet which Mint tradition associates with Newton.

Below. Queen Anne five guineas of 1703, struck from gold captured at Vigo.

With the routine administrative arrangements of the Mint he seems to have been generally content and he left them largely undisturbed. Occasionally at odds with his colleagues, 'with whom I sometimes find it difficult to agree', he seems to have been happiest in the search for precedent, as in the disputes with the Tower garrison when it encroached on the ancient privileges of the Mint. But if he proved no innovator, it needs to be said that, in contrast to the indolent and sometimes eccentric behaviour of predecessors such as Thomas Neale, he brought industry and integrity to the Master's post.

Similarly, he made no decisive contribution to the development of the minting process. Though a stranger in the Coining Press Room, he was nevertheless familiar with the mechanical processes, and more particularly with the theory and practice of assaying, reflecting a long sustained personal interest in alchemy. This was at its most evident in the controversy over the gold trial plate of 1707, where he was able to demonstrate that the plate had been made too fine and that the consequent assertion of the Pyx jury that the coins were below standard was an unwarranted slur on the workmanship of the Mint. Above all, he was concerned that coins should be made more uniform in weight and fineness, and it is a tribute to this great man that his successor

Right. Obverse and reverse punches for the five guineas of 1703. The missing details were added by hand to each die.

Below. Muffle furnace, said to have been used by Newton.

Right. Central portion of the disputed gold trial plate of 1707.

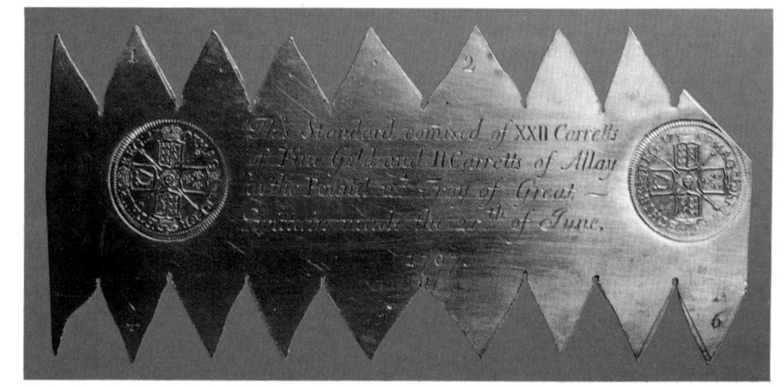

could claim in 1730 that the Mint's coins were the most accurately struck in the world.

Above. Nest of Mint weights, prepared in 1707 and known as Queen Anne's Pile.

The Eighteenth Century

The Mint in Newton's time remained between the inner and outer walls of the Tower, running as in the reign of Elizabeth in a narrow horseshoe on the three sides not bounded by the river. A paved street, still known as Mint Street, separated two lines of buildings which, in Sir John Craig's dramatic description, 'were largely of wood; the chief of them were two-storied; most were crazy with age, held up by timber shores and pinned together with clamps of iron.' Well might a foreign visitor in 1710 express surprise that handsome coins could emanate from such wretched buildings.

Between 1728 and 1731 the mill rooms were rebuilt and re-equipped, 'having been for some years supported only by Props, & being now in so ruinous a condition that the Moneyers cannot work therein without great danger to themselves & the treasure they are entrusted with....' Additional mill rooms and a new press room were erected later in the century, but on the whole Mint organisation left much to be desired. Many of the senior officers delegated the performance of their duties to hired deputies; few bothered to live in their official houses within the Tower; the

Below. Plan of the Tower Mint, drawn up by William Allingham in 1701.

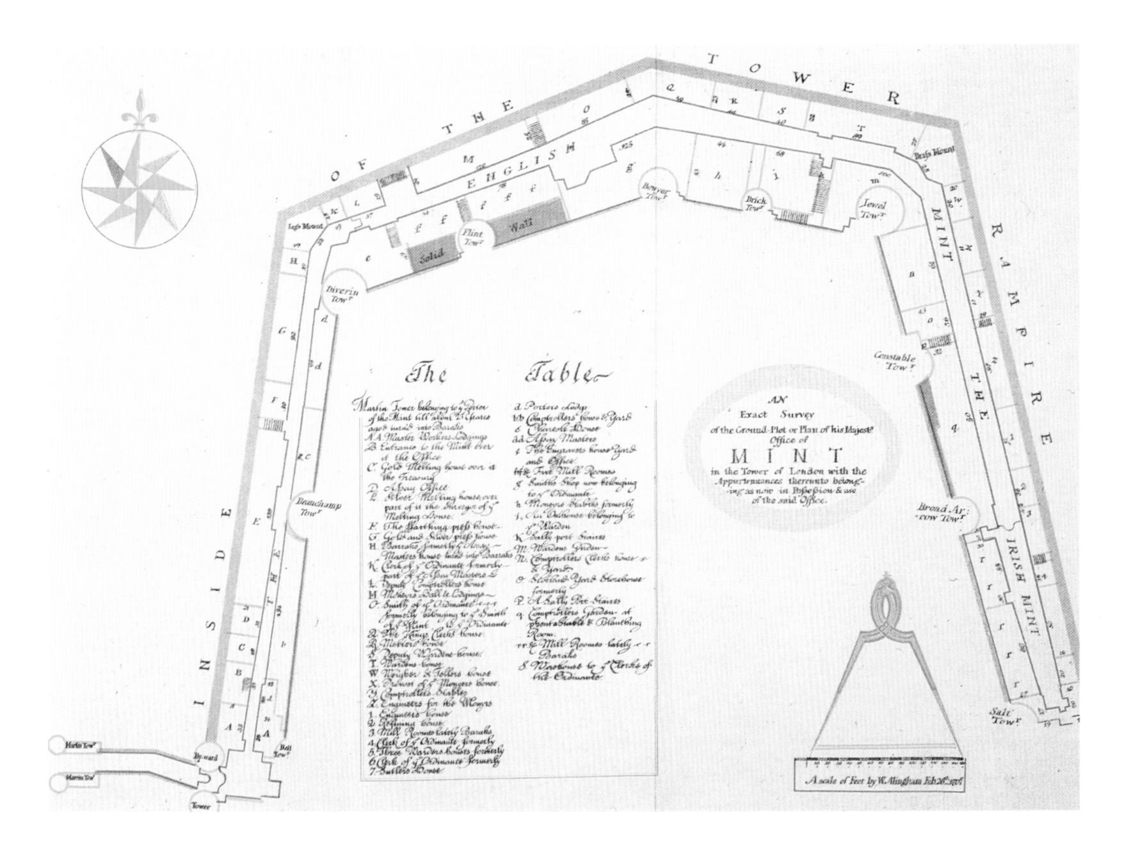

Above. John Conduitt, husband of Newton's step-niece and Master of the Mint from 1727 to 1737. (Actual size 58mm)

organisation, with its independent officers checking on each other, lacked unity and purpose; and the neglect of the Government contributed to a general lethargy. Only among the assayers, where there were men of the ability of Joseph Harris and Stanesby Alchorne, was the story more creditable.

The decline in the Mint reflected a decline in the coinage itself. Though gold, principally in the form of guineas, continued to be a regular feature of Mint output, the striking of silver coin dwindled as the century advanced and there were also long intervals when the coining of copper came to a stop. This paucity of minting, the result of economic and other factors quite outside the control of the Mint, could not fail to be bad for the morale and skill of the Mint officers.

By the end of the century Matthew Boulton's private mint at Soho in Birmingham was undoubtedly far superior to the Tower Mint. Boulton's partner, the inventor James Watt, had succeeded by means of a rotative steam engine in harnessing steam power to the coining process. This enabled coins to be produced far faster than was possible at the Mint in the Tower and also permitted a greater uniformity in size and diameter. The entrepreneur Boulton was a man of influence, whose cause was championed by men such as the Earl of Liverpool and Sir Joseph Banks. So when the copper coinage was at last restored in 1797 it was Boulton who, much to the dismay of the moneyers in the Tower, managed to win for Soho the contract for the new cartwheel twopences and pence.

Above. From the bookplate of the Mint assayer, Stanesby Alchorne.

Above. Striking coins in the Tower Mint. From the *Universal Magazine*, 1750.

With the Tower Mint's fortunes at a low ebb, reform was at last seriously contemplated. In 1798 a powerful Committee of the Privy Council was charged with consideration of 'the state of

Above. Medal of Thomas Howard, Earl of Effingham, Master of the Mint from 1784 to 1789.

Above. Medal of Matthew Boulton. The circles and numbers on the reverse refer to the rates of output of Boulton's presses. (Actual size 40.5mm)
Right, cart.wheel penny of 1797, struck at Boulton's Soho Mint.

Above. A view of one of the coining press rooms in the Tower, c. 1809.

the Coins of this Kingdom, and the present Establishment and Constitution of His Majesty's Mint.' Evidence was taken from the Mint officers, and surveys of the Mint and its processes were commissioned from the engineer John Rennie, the chemist Charles Hatchett and the physicist Henry Cavendish. Advice was sought from Boulton himself, and the Committee must have quickly formed the view that the mint machinery was of an 'ancient and imperfect Construction.'

Above. Mint Office seal, showing the White Tower. (Actual size 28mm across)

Right. Last seal of the Mint Corporation, c. 1709. Removed from the Mint in the nineteenth century and subsequently recovered from a pawnbroker's shop. (Actual size 61mm)

TOWER HILL

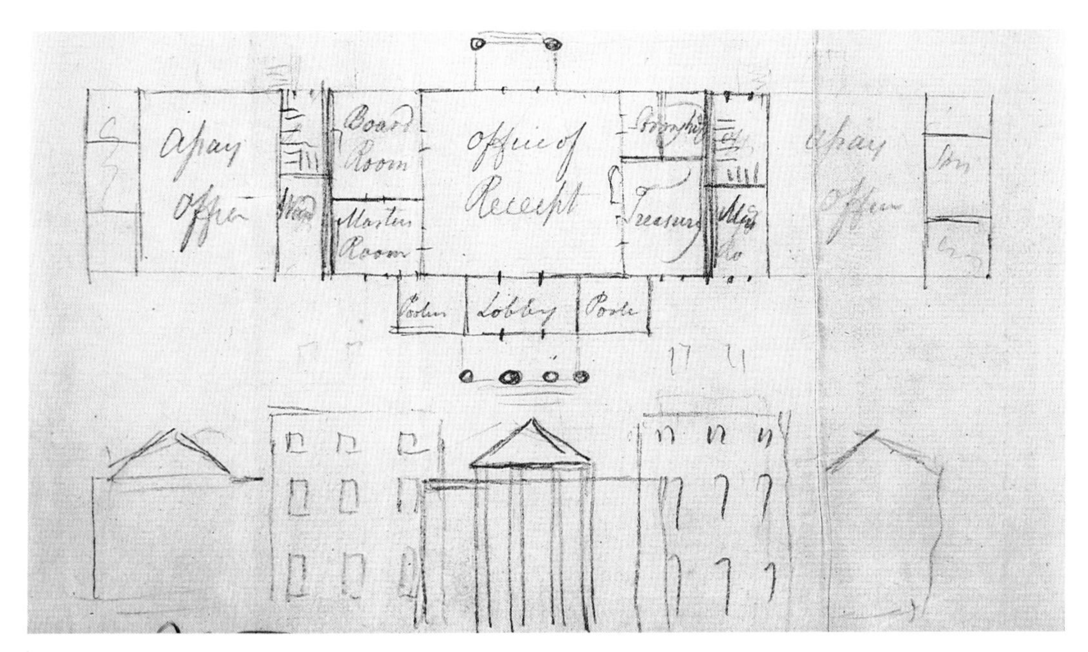

Above. Rough sketch inserted in a copy of the Mint officers' report of 16 November 1804 on their requirements for the new mint.

Below. George III half-guinea of 1809. One of the last coins to be struck in the Tower.

The Move to Tower Hill

Action did not follow immediately. It was not until 1804 that the Committee reminded itself of the investigations of 1798 and delivered the opinion that the Mint ought to be furnished with 'the most improved Engines and Machines of all kinds applicable to the fabrication of Money that can be obtained in this or any other Country.'

Further consultations took place and it was soon agreed that the Mint should be equipped with Boulton's machinery. The Board of Ordnance, however, declared that not only could no further space be found in the Tower to accommodate the new machinery but that part of the existing site, miserably unattractive though it might be, was 'absolutely wanted' for the defence of the Tower and the safety of its stores. The Committee was conscious that no other place could be as secure as the Tower, but comforted itself with the thought that the distant Bank of England, with its larger holdings of precious metal, seemed safe enough. A fresh site in any case promised extra space and also meant that the existing mint could continue in operation while the new mint was being built. These seemed solid advantages to be set against the rather lower cost of adapting the buildings in the Tower and the Committee accordingly decided in favour of a new mint on a new site.

The site recommended by John Rennie and the Mint surveyor, James Johnson, was on Little Tower Hill, only a few hundred yards from the Tower. It was a site occupied by tobacco warehouses, conveniently about to become redundant, and much earlier by the great Cistercian abbey of Eastminster. Preliminary

Above. One of James Johnson's original drawings, and *right*, view of the new mint from the Tower moat.

Above. John Rennie. Detail from a medal.

Below. Copper coin for Prince of Wales's Island, 1810. This was the first coinage to be struck in the new Tower Hill mint.

work began in 1805 and Rennie reported in November that the foundations were preparing and 'the works will soon be in a state to require constant and regular attention.' A contract for the supply of machinery was signed with Boulton in July 1806, and when three senior Mint officers visited Soho a year later they found a considerable part of the machinery already packed for despatch. The buildings in which it was to be housed, however, were not yet ready and it was February 1810 before the machinery was nearly all in place, though even then the 'Great Rolling Mill' still had to await the completion of a tunnel from the Tower 'ditch.' Finally in April 1810 the moneyers were authorised to try out the machinery on a coinage of copper for the settlement at Prince of Wales's Island, now Penang.

Removal from the Tower was fairly leisurely. In the early summer of 1810 one of the mill rooms was surrendered and made available for the custody of Ordnance stores. But it was May 1811, with the Weighing Room and Offices of Receipt in the 'great Building' at last capable of occupation, before the Pyx boxes, books and other office items were ordered to be transferred. In July the guardroom was deemed sufficiently complete for the reception of the military guard, but work still remained to be done on some of the dwelling houses in the new mint. Not until August 1812, when accommodation was urgently required for the 'temporary reception of the wounded and sick soldiers lately arrived from India', were keys to the old mint in the Tower eventually relinquished.

Above. The main building and the gatehouses. From a drawing by T. H. Shepherd, 1830.

The New Tower Hill Mint

The new mint, built at a cost of some £300,000, stood in sharp contrast to its rather ramshackle predecessor. The main building, designed by James Johnson and finished by his successor Robert Smirke, was handsome and dignified, achieving a 'modest grandeur'. It was intended as a residential block, with dwellings for such senior officers as the Deputy Master and the King's Assay Master, but there was space on the ground floor for the Pyx Office and for stronghold accommodation. Behind this building, and separated from it by an open quadrangle, were the buildings which housed the new machinery. Custom-built for the purpose, they permitted a logical flow of work from one process to the next; and to the Mint officers, accustomed to the cramped conditions of the Tower, it all seemed 'stupendous and beautiful', 'simple, beautiful and effectual'. It was, in short, a mint worthy of the designation Royal now increasingly applied to it.

Above. Bank of England silver token for eighteen-pence, 1811.

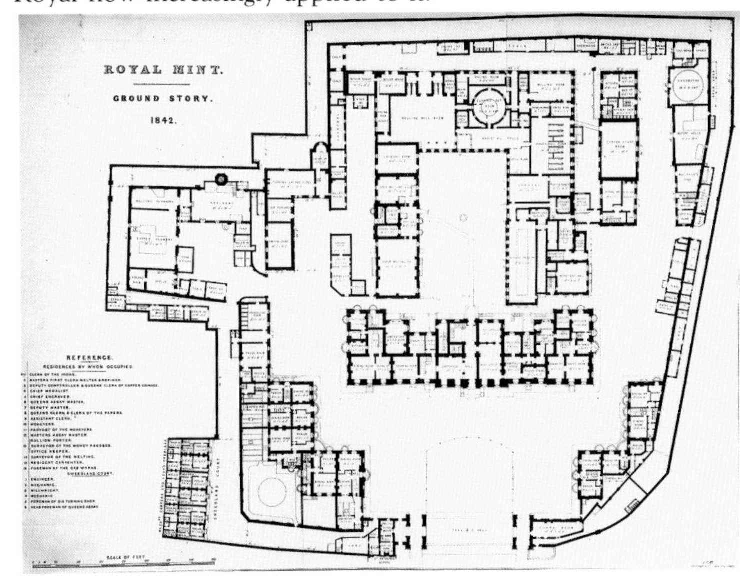

Right. Ground plan of the Tower Hill mint, 1842.

Above. French twenty-franc piece, 1815. Struck at Tower Hill for the payment of Wellington's army in France.

Right. Reverse of the medal awarded to the victorious troops at Waterloo.

Below. A Boulton coining press at Tower Hill. From an engraving in the *Saturday Magazine*, 1836.

Right. One of the blank-cutting machines installed by Boulton at Tower Hill.

Above. The gold sovereign was revived in 1817.

Below. The new silver coinage was completed in 1818 with the striking of a handsome crown piece, designed by Pistrucci.

In many respects it was a carbon copy of the Soho Mint and sadly Matthew Boulton, its true founder, did not live to see it completed. It was in the rolling room where Boulton's machinery made its first major impact on the coining process, with two ponderous lines of shafting running from end to end of the room transmitting power from a 30 hp steam engine to the rolling mills. In the blank-cutting room, a round room about thirty feet in diameter, twelve cutting out presses were arranged in a circle around a heavy upright shaft, which supported a large horizontal flywheel with twelve cams to operate the presses. The coins were struck in a long room, down the middle of which eight massive coining presses, separated by columns of oak, were arranged in a straight line. The central screw of each press culminated at the top in two arms, and the eight presses were operated by a 10 hp steam engine. They were each capable of striking about 60 coins a minute and when all of them were at work the noise was deafening.

Right. Benedetto Pistrucci's dies for the medal to commemorate the Battle of Waterloo. Too large to harden at more than 5 inches in diameter, the dies could not be used to strike medals.

The Tower Hill mint was quickly into its stride. Now that the Government at last had its expensive new mint, it was naturally determined that all its coinage requirements, both for home and overseas, should be undertaken there. The summer of 1811 therefore saw the start of a large production of silver tokens for the Bank of England, while the exigencies of war with Napoleon explains the striking of Anglo-Hanoverian gold coins, of French twenty-franc pieces, and of medals for the victorious troops at Waterloo. An unusually energetic Master arrived in 1814 with the appointment of William Wellesley Pole, an elder brother of the Duke of Wellington. With great skill he organised the introduction of a new gold and silver coinage after Waterloo, and his employment of the talented Italian Benedetto Pistrucci bore witness to his intention that 'we may not only have to boast of the most beautiful and correct Mint machinery in the world, but that we may stand equally unrivalled for the perfect form and exquisite taste of our several coins.'

Below. Pistrucci's portrait of William Wellesley Pole, Master of the Mint from 1814 to 1823. (Actual size 50mm)

Administrative Reform

The new mint on Tower Hill inherited the existing staff and some of the bad habits of the old mint in the Tower. The Master remained a political appointee, certain of the officers still employed deputies, and others used their official status as a means of generating private income. Much of the work continued to be performed under contract, with the actual task of minting, for instance, still in the hands of the self-styled Company of Moneyers. Yet the Mint nevertheless contrived to produce what were then probably the most technically perfect coins in the world. And it is possible to see a sense of community developing in the houses and buildings behind the high boundary wall, with son succeeding father and with families like the Wyons and the Beckwiths linked by marriage. Many spent the whole of their working lives in the Mint: John Wisker, one of the workmen employed by the moneyers in 1823, had been first engaged by them in 1774; and when in 1849 the admirable James Morrison at last contemplated retirement from the post of Deputy Master it was 'after 56 years of constant duties in the Mint.' Not all was sweetness and light, and the rivalry in the Engraving Department between William Wyon and Benedetto Pistrucci was a matter of open comment in the press.

Above. Sir James Morrison, Deputy Master 1803 - 1850. From a painting by G.Clint.

Below. William Wyon, Chief Engraver 1828 - 1851. A medallic portrait by his son Leonard, also a Mint engraver. (Actual size 55mm)

Below. Seal of the Company of Moneyers. Taken from a brass plate attached to the side of a box of weights.

Right. A balance constructed in 1826 by John Field, Weigher and Teller of the Mint.

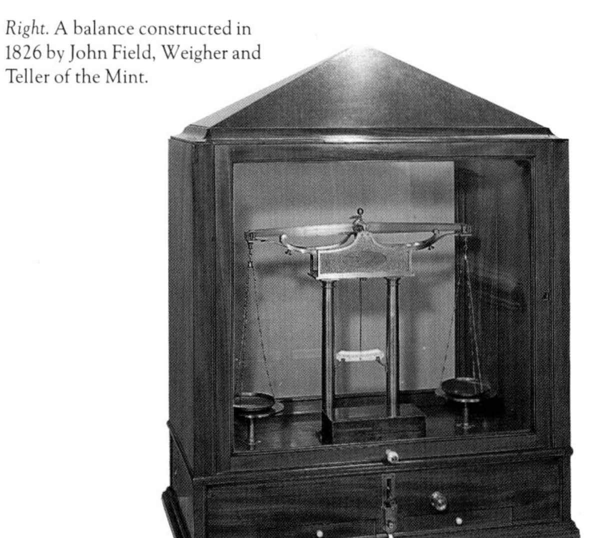

The process of reform was started by Wellesley Pole. He did not, however, disturb the contract system and it was growing criticism of the moneyers which prompted the appointment of a Select Committee in 1837. The work of the Committee was frustrated by the termination of the Parliamentary session, but it was clear that something had to be done about the 'complicated,

Above. The arrival of Chinese booty at the Mint. From the *Illustrated London News, 1843.*

Below. Medal recording the visit in 1853 of the Prince of Wales, later Edward VII.

difficult, operose, and unintelligible' organisation of the Mint. Further investigation followed in 1848, when a Royal Commission was appointed to consider the 'Constitution, Management, and Expense of Our Royal Mint.' The moneyers, through their provost, Sir Jasper Atkinson, declined to disclose their profits and Gilbert Mathison and Henry Bingley, Melter and Queen's Assay Master respectively, were likewise reluctant to give the Commission all the information for which it asked. Not surprisingly, the Commission recommended the following year that the contract system should be abandoned, that there should be a full-time officer responsible for the running of the entire mint, and that the old Indenture between Master and Monarch should be replaced by a more precise and systematic code.

It was, said *The Times*, a 'vigorous and well arranged' report and action quickly followed. The moneyers, five in number, were given notice and, handsomely compensated, left the Mint in July 1851. The Melter and the Queen's Assay Master were dealt with in the same uncomplicated fashion, leaving the functions of the Coining and Melting Departments to be undertaken by staff directly employed by the Government. All now came under the control of the Master and the separate empires of quasi-independent officers became a thing of the past. In its organisation, therefore, the Mint came to resemble a fairly typical Government Department, unease with the Mastership of the distinguished chemist Thomas Graham (1855-1869) causing the process to culminate in 1870 with the appointment of the Chancellor of the Exchequer as ex officio Master of the Mint. Day-to-day administration then devolved on to the Deputy Master, who was and remains a permanent civil servant.

Above. Sir Charles Fremantle, Deputy Master 1868 - 1894.

Right. The Gold Melting House and Rolling Room c. 1900, from a contemporary set of postcards.

Below. Victorian bronze penny. In 1860 heavy copper coins were replaced by lighter and more convenient coins in bronze.

The establishment was not large and the 100 or so members of the staff in 1870 must have seemed thinly scattered in the extensive buildings at Tower Hill. Indeed, a new and very able Deputy Master, Charles Fremantle, would have preferred a smaller site nearer the centre of London and during the 1870s much time and energy was devoted to the question of moving the Mint. Until the future location could be settled, Fremantle was unable to proceed with the installation of much-needed new machinery and in particular of up-to-date coining presses. Boulton's equipment, so highly regarded sixty years before, had come to seem 'clamorous and turbulent,' and Fremantle complained that he was asked to produce the coinage of the Empire with machinery more antiquated than that of any mint in Europe, including Constantinople.

Eventually the question of a new site was abandoned, for it was found possible during a period of low demand for coin to suspend minting for several months in 1882 and to make the

necessary alterations at Tower Hill. The gold melting house was extended, a new rolling room was constructed, and in the cutting room the old Boulton machines were replaced by neater and smaller presses from Heaton's of Birmingham, arranged in two lines down opposite sides of the room. In the Coining Press Room the massive Boulton screw presses were replaced by a double line of Heaton presses, standing back to back and straddling a central underground shaft from which they drew their power. A little faster but much quieter than the Boulton presses, the Heaton lever presses were capable of producing 75,000 coins an hour when all were at work.

Time quickly demonstrated the wisdom of retaining a large site and of expanding capacity. Output now began to climb dramatically and an annual production of only 24 million coins in 1870 had risen to 100 million by the end of the century.

Above. Policemen at the Mint entrance, March 1898.

Right. Cutting and Press Rooms c. 1900, showing the Heaton machinery installed in 1882.

Below. Florin of Edward VII (1901 - 1910).

Cutting Room, The Royal Mint.

Press Room, The Royal Mint.

Above. Medal awarded for service during the Boer War.

Below. Gold sovereign of 1914, struck at the Sydney Branch of the Royal Mint.

Below. Reverse of Australian florin, 1911.

The Mint in 1914

In 1914, at the outbreak of the First World War, the Royal Mint could be reckoned as one of the great institutions of the British Empire. First of all it managed an Imperial currency, since the British coins which it produced circulated in various parts of the Empire as well as at home. Moreover, many Colonies which had adopted distinctive coinages of their own looked to the Royal Mint for the regular supply of their coins, and this trend had accelerated in the opening years of the twentieth century with the introduction of special coinages for British East Africa, British West Africa and Australia. Overseas branch mints, controlled from Tower Hill, had been set up in Australia at Sydney, Melbourne and Perth, and a fourth branch had recently been opened in Ottawa in 1908. A fifth branch was briefly in operation at Bombay in 1918, while a sixth was established at Pretoria in 1923. These branches were empowered to strike Imperial gold coins and such was their importance that their combined output of sovereigns was virtually as great as that of the Royal Mint itself.

Most official gallantry and campaign medals, with the notable exception of the Victoria Cross, were struck at Tower Hill and there was also a limited production of prize and commemorative medals. The engraving of seals, occasionally in the past an additional task for the Mint engravers, had become an official responsibility in 1901, when the Deputy Master was appointed ex officio Engraver of His Majesty's Seals, thereby involving the Mint in the engraving of many ministerial and colonial seals but most spectacularly in the design and preparation of the Great Seal of the Realm. Other new responsibilities were assumed in 1910, when the Mint took over the production of the dies required by the Inland Revenue for embossing cheques, transfers and other legal documents and of the dies and plates required for the printing of adhesive stamps for postage and fiscal purposes. With banknotes, however, it continued to have nothing to do.

By 1914 the staff of the Mint had grown to nearly 300, split between the Mint Office, the Operative Department and the Assay Department. About three dozen, responsible for the issue of coin as well as for more normal clerical duties, worked in the Mint Office under the Chief Clerk. Most of the staff were employed in the Operative Department in self-contained sections which generated their own traditions and sense of loyalty but which came under the general supervision of a Superintendent and three Assistant Superintendents. The Assay Department, in the charge of a Chemist & Assayer and with a staff of less than a dozen, was the smallest of the three branches. Yet it was responsible for the accuracy with which the coins were made and enjoyed an international reputation, the work of Sir William Chandler Roberts-Austen and then of Sir Thomas Rose placing the Mint for more

4 OTTAWA (1908 - 1931)

5 BOMBAY (1918 - 1919)

PRETORIA (1923 - 1941) 6

PERTH (1899 - 1970) 3

MELBOURNE (1872 - 1968) 2

1 SYDNEY (1855 - 1926)

Right. Overseas branches of the Royal Mint.

Right. Great Seal of Edward VII, designed by the Mint engraver G.W. De Saulles. (Actual size 154mm)

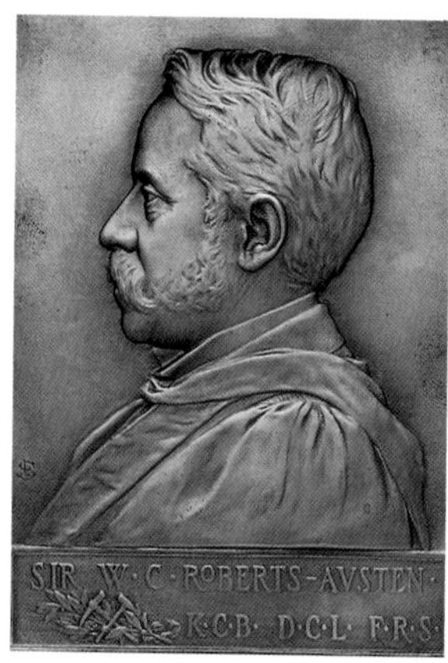

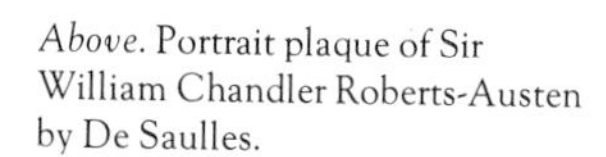

Above. Portrait plaque of Sir William Chandler Roberts-Austen by De Saulles.

Right. Three senior officers photographed at the Royal Mint in 1898. From the left Edward Rigg (Chief Clerk), Horace Seymour (Deputy Master) and Robert Hill (Superintendent).

Right. Automatic counting machines, clumsy but time-saving, were introduced in the 1890s.

Right. The new Rolling Room, completed in 1904.

Below. This watch-case shows that members of the staff away on war service were not forgotten by their colleagues.

than a quarter of a century within the circle of the world's great scientific institutions.

It was a mint, too, in which change and alteration was becoming continuous, the pace noticeably quickening after Edward Rigg became Superintendent in 1898. Work commenced in 1899 on a new two-storey building to house the Medal Department; the Cutting and Annealing Rooms were re-organised in 1901; a new Rolling Room was erected in 1904; in 1908 a new Mechanics' Shop was constructed; in 1910 three-storied buildings were put in hand for the stamp plate department; in 1911 the new Silver Melting House was completed; and the following year saw the completion of the Gold Melting House. The use of electricity increased dramatically and in 1907 the old steam engines were finally replaced. Another consequence of the extensive alterations was that dwelling houses were taken over, so that fewer and fewer members of the staff now lived on the site. The success of these changes in promoting greater efficiency and a more rapid out-turn of coin may be seen in the achievement of an unprecedented output of 250 million coins a year during the First World War.

Peace and War

The Mint of the 1920s and 1930s was dominated by Sir Robert Johnson. A clear-sighted man of action, he was appointed Deputy Master in 1922 and quickly made an impact on a mint tired by the demands of the War.

A major concern, in common with manufacturing industry generally, was to keep the Mint fully occupied and its skilled staff intact as business activity slackened after the War. To this end Johnson enthusiastically launched the Mint on a course which has shaped much of its subsequent history by deliberately seeking coinage orders from foreign countries. Instead of merely being content to accept orders from the largely tied market of the Empire, Johnson went out of his way to pick up work wherever it could be found. In the disturbed political and economic conditions of the post-War world there were fortunately many opportunities to apply the new policy and, sometimes with the help of personal

Above. Sir Robert Johnson, Deputy Master 1922 - 1938.

Above. In 1920 sterling silver, 'the old right standard of the monies of silver of England', was replaced by an inferior alloy containing only 500 parts per 1000 of silver.

Right. The Weighing Room in the 1920s, showing the automatic balances for weighing gold and silver coins.

Right. The Reducing Room in the 1930s.

Above. Silver half-rouble of 1924, struck by the Royal Mint for the Soviet Union.

visits from Johnson, orders were received from countries such as Bulgaria, Estonia, Greece, Guatemala, Iraq, Latvia, Lithuania, Poland, Rumania and, surprisingly, the Soviet Union. These successes secured for the Mint a foothold in areas like the Middle East and Latin America which were to provide regular orders in the years to come. In addition Johnson was determined that as countries such as New Zealand and Southern Rhodesia abandoned the use of British coin so their new coinages should also be struck in London.

Nor were medals neglected. The Medal Department was rebuilt, and the variety of medals and plaques struck for the British Empire Exhibition in 1924 clearly signalled the Mint's interest in expanding medal production. To raise the level of medallic art, young artists were encouraged and a new generation of artists, among them George Kruger Gray, Percy Metcalfe, Humphrey Paget, and Langford Jones, received a steady stream of commissions from

Above. Latvian coins struck by the Royal Mint in the 1920s.

Above. Commemorative crown piece for the Silver Jubilee of George V, 1935. *Opposite*, striking souvenir medals for the Jubilee.

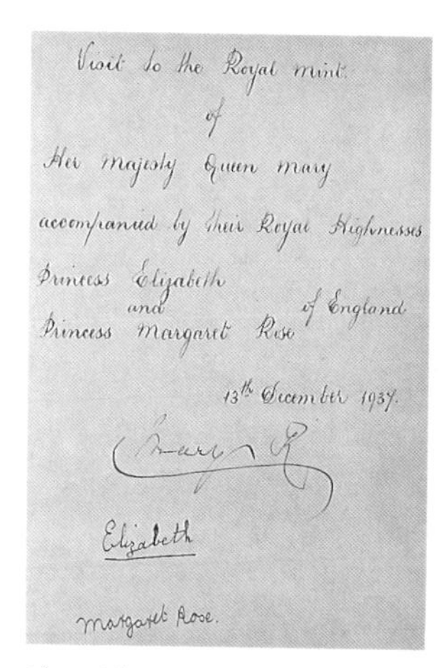

Visit to the Royal Mint
of
Her Majesty Queen Mary
accompanied by Their Royal Highnesses
Princess Elizabeth
and
Princess Margaret Rose
of England

13th December 1937.

Mary R

Elizabeth

Margaret Rose.

Above. The Queen, as Princess Elizabeth, visited the Mint in 1937.

Above. Sir John Craig, Deputy Master 1938 - 1949.
(Actual size 56.5mm)

Right. The employment of women in the Coining Press Room during the Second World War.

the Mint. An independent and influential Advisory Committee was set up with the approval of King George V to examine new designs and to offer advice to the Deputy Master, who recognised that a permanent civil servant ought not to act unaided as an arbiter of public taste.

Johnson died in 1938 and it was left to his successor, the scholarly Sir John Craig, to guide the Mint through the Second World War. Output increased to nearly 700 million coins a year during the War, double the pre-War average and achieved in spite of the disruption of power and material supplies, the posting of men to the Services and, as in the First World War, the diversion of skilled resources to high precision munitions work. For the first time, in 1941, women entered the factory to operate cutting presses, marking machines, coining presses and overlooking tables. To increase the capacity of the Mint and to secure the coinage against the effects of any long term stoppage at Tower Hill, an auxiliary mint was set up in one of the Pinewood Cinema Studios near Iver Heath in Buckinghamshire. Staff and machinery were transferred there from Tower Hill and the temporary mint remained in operation from June 1941 until September 1945, producing some 430 million United Kingdom and overseas coins.

In an area so close to the docks some damage was inevitable at Tower Hill. The Mint received its share of high explosive and incendiary bombs, and sadly in December 1940 three members of the staff were killed during an air raid. Windows and roofs in the factory were wrecked by enemy action, but fortunately the fabric of the main building suffered only superficial damage.

Right. Wartime damage to the front of the main building.

Below and Across. A variety of passes used by Mint staff at Tower Hill.

Expansion at Tower Hill

The shortages and general austerity which followed the War had their effect on the Mint. The use of silver had at last to be abandoned for the British coinage and the adoption of cupro-nickel in its place necessitated the introduction of high frequency induction furnaces and of heavy breakdown rolling mills to cope with the thick strips of cupro-nickel. Supplies of nickel proved difficult for a time and there were persistent complaints of a shortage of shillings. There was diversion of a kind for the hard-pressed staff in 1951 when the Mint installed a coining press at the South Bank exhibition for the Festival of Britain and sold commemorative crown pieces across the counter to an eager public.

As conditions eased, the Mint again took up with enthusiasm the challenge of the export market and output increased dramatically from the late 1950s. Large orders were received from newly-independent countries in Africa, such as Ghana and Nigeria, and these continued into the 1960s as more

Above. The first United Kingdom coins struck in cupro-nickel were dated 1947.

Above. Coins of a new reign, 1953.

Right. Molten metal being poured from a furnace and *below,* strip being rolled in a heavy breakdown mill.

Below. One of the coins struck for Ghana, 1958.

Above. Medallion struck at the Mint stand at the British Exhibition in New York, 1960. The obverse shows the Mint Crest, whose origins can be traced back to the 1820s.

Above and Below. General Service Medal, 1962.

Above Right. Coins being inspected on overlooking tables.

countries achieved independence, among them Kenya, Tanzania, Uganda and Zambia. Decimalisation accounted for welcome orders from Australia and New Zealand, and other major customers included the Philippines and Ethiopia, both countries which had not previously placed orders with the Mint. Despite stiff competition the Mint succeeded in capturing over 75 per cent of the available trade in the non-Communist world and rather more than half its output went overseas. In 1964 production for the first time exceeded 1000 million coins in a year, and in 1966 the Mint secured a place among the first winners of the Queen's Award to Industry.

These results could only be achieved by more or less continuous patching and renovation, so that by the 1960s little of the original mint remained apart from the administrative building in the front. In truth Tower Hill had become something of a rabbit warren and conditions must have seemed somewhat Dickensian to

Above. Royal Mint messenger's badge, adopted in 1950. (Actual size 28.5mm across)

Right. A view across the crowded roofs of the factory.

Below. Reverse of the Churchill crown, 1965. The portrait is by Oscar Nemon.

the constant stream of visitors who toured the factory. Melting capacity was increased, additional and faster coining presses were purchased, electronic counting machines were introduced, a hydraulic press facilitated the making of dies, and an X ray fluorescence spectrometer was installed to speed up the analysis of metals. Medals and seals continued to be made by the Mint but postage work had declined since the 1930s with the adoption of the new process of photogravure. A site that in 1870 had housed some 100 staff now had to cope with well over ten times that number; but though the staff had increased so dramatically, the old sense of family and comradeship survived in the factory, and there was friendly rivalry between the different rooms and sections.

All in all, it was a successful and thriving mint which welcomed the Queen on the afternoon of 8 June 1966.

Right. Cyril Tomlinson explaining the operation of a reducing machine to the Queen. The Master of the Mint, James Callaghan, is on the right.

Below. The main building at Tower Hill, photographed in 1979.

LLANTRISANT

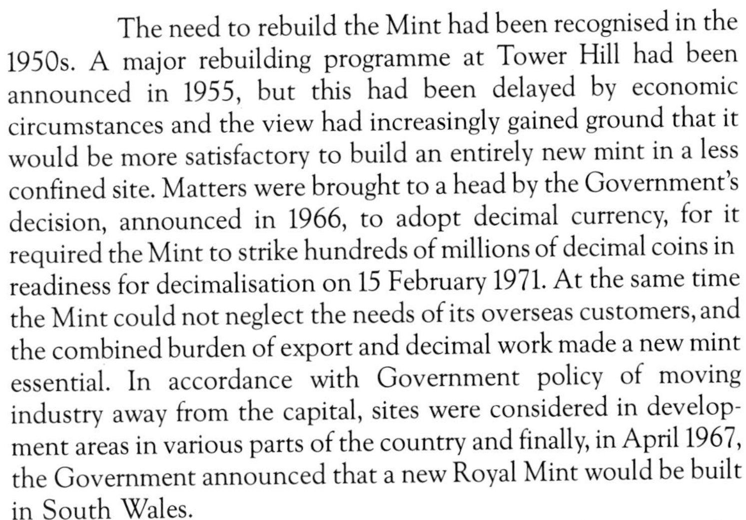

The Move to Llantrisant

The need to rebuild the Mint had been recognised in the 1950s. A major rebuilding programme at Tower Hill had been announced in 1955, but this had been delayed by economic circumstances and the view had increasingly gained ground that it would be more satisfactory to build an entirely new mint in a less confined site. Matters were brought to a head by the Government's decision, announced in 1966, to adopt decimal currency, for it required the Mint to strike hundreds of millions of decimal coins in readiness for decimalisation on 15 February 1971. At the same time the Mint could not neglect the needs of its overseas customers, and the combined burden of export and decimal work made a new mint essential. In accordance with Government policy of moving industry away from the capital, sites were considered in development areas in various parts of the country and finally, in April 1967, the Government announced that a new Royal Mint would be built in South Wales.

The site chosen was at Llantrisant, ten miles or so to the north-west of Cardiff and set in rolling green countryside on the edge of the Rhondda Valley. Work began in August 1967 on the construction of two large concrete-clad buildings, one for the

Above. The new decimal bronze coins, mostly struck at Llantrisant.

Right. 'I had the frightening pleasure of turning the first sod, in a monster weighing 37 tons, on 7th August': J.H. James (later Sir Jack James), Deputy Master of the Mint in 1967.

Far right. Photograph taken on 7 March 1968, showing progress on the Annealing and Pickling Block.

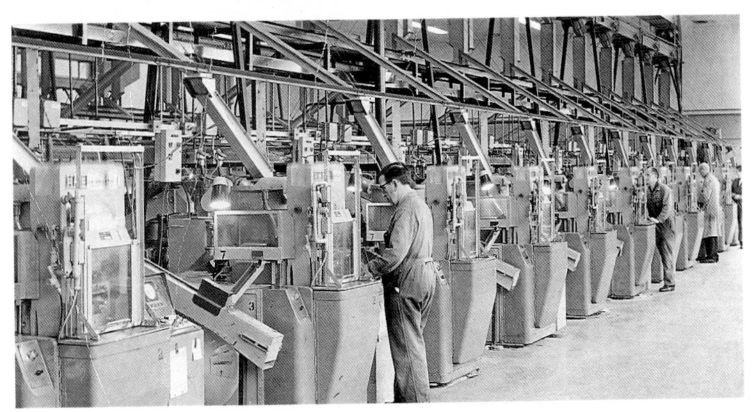

Right. A line of coining presses in the new mint, 1969.

Right. The Queen watches coins being counted during her visit to Llantrisant on 17 December 1968. The Master of the Mint, Roy Jenkins, looks on.

treatment of blanks and the other for the striking of those blanks. This first phase was opened by the Queen in December 1968, when she switched on the coining presses to begin production of decimal bronze coins. During 1969 the new mint, with its modern facilities for the bulk handling of blanks and the automatic feeding of lines of coining presses, achieved weekly rates of output in excess of 50 million coins, or twice as much in a week as a century earlier the Mint had produced in a year. Blanks were supplied from Tower Hill and by outside contractors and, as planned, the new mint was responsible for the bulk of the stockpile of decimal bronze coins.

After the decimal change-over had been successfully negotiated, a second phase of building work was undertaken at Llantrisant. Its main feature was a large melting, rolling and blanking unit, in which was installed one of the most up-to-date foundries in the world for the continuous casting of non-ferrous metals. Another substantial building provided accommodation for

Below. For security reasons plastic tokens are used instead of coins within the Mint.

Right. Work in progress on the Melting, Rolling and Blanking unit, 8 November 1972.

the Engraving, Die and Assay Departments and for the special section responsible for the striking of proof coins for sale to collectors. An office building and a police post were also constructed, and the new mint now occupies a total area of some thirty acres.

Until the second phase of building at Llantrisant had been completed, the old mint at Tower Hill continued in operation. After 1972, however, few coins were struck in London and, once the new mint had become largely self-sufficient with the commissioning of the additional plant, production in London of blanks and coin was brought to an end. The last coin, a gold sovereign, was struck at Tower Hill with due ceremony in November 1975, by which time many of the staff had already left. In 1978 Marketing and Sales staff, who formed most of the small remnant at Tower Hill, moved across London to office accommodation in Victoria; and finally in 1980 the last of the staff, along with the Mint's historic numismatic collection, left London for Llantrisant.

Above. This sovereign, dated 1974, was the last coin struck at Tower Hill, 10 November 1975.

Below. Medal marking the end of production at Tower Hill. The designs are by Robert Elderton, one of the Mint engravers. (Actual size 53.5mm)

Right. The ceremonial striking of the last coin.

Below. The new mint after the completion of the second phase of building.

Minting Processes at Llantrisant

The first stage in the coining process is the melting of the constituent metals, usually copper, nickel, zinc or tin, in the appropriate proportions for the alloy required. At Tower Hill this was essentially a small-scale affair, with the molten metal being poured into vertical moulds, but the new mint has a continuous casting unit in operation twenty-four hours a day. By this system, virgin metals and process scrap are melted in primary electric furnaces and, when examination of a sample by X-ray fluorescence spectrometry has confirmed that the alloy is correct, the molten metal is transferred to holding furnaces. From the holding furnace it is drawn horizontally and continuously in the form of a strip about 200 millimetres wide and 15 millimetres thick, with cutting equipment built into the casting line dividing the strip into manageable 10 metre lengths weighing some 200 kilograms each.

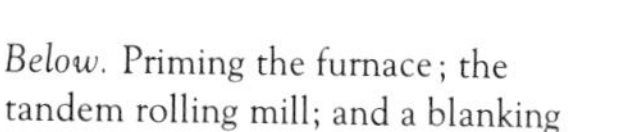

Below. Priming the furnace; the tandem rolling mill; and a blanking press.

Right. Continuous casting.

A tandem rolling mill begins the process of reducing the metal to coin thickness. If, as with nickel-brass, intermediate annealing or softening is necessary, the strip is passed slowly through a furnace at a temperature of about 650°C. During the rolling process, for ease of handling, five of the cast lengths are welded together to create a large coil weighing about one tonne. A finishing mill then completes the task, its rolls reversible so that the coil of strip can pass backwards and forwards until it is reduced to the thickness required. From the finished coils blank discs are punched out in large presses at rates of up to 14,000 blanks a minute and collected in drums. The scrap metal, known for centuries as scissel, is passed back to the furnace for re-melting.

The drums of blanks are then transferred from the Melting, Rolling and Blanking Unit to the Annealing and Pickling Block. Here they are fed from large hoppers into gas-fired annealing furnaces where they are softened by being heated to high temperature, 850°C in the case of cupro-nickel and 750°C for bronze. After cooling they are passed to automatic pickling barrels where stains are removed by a solution of sulphuric acid and, after a final washing in tartaric acid, they are rinsed in water and dried by hot air. Most blanks then go to the marking machines, where they are rolled under pressure down a narrow groove to force the metal inwards in order to thicken the edge of the blank. This then makes it easier to give the coin a raised rim to protect it from wear and to enable coins to be stacked in piles.

The final process is the stamping on the blanks of the obverse and reverse designs and, when required, the milling on the edge. These operations are carried out simultaneously in a coining

Above. Blanks being transferred to pickling barrels.

Right. Line of modern coining presses.

press, into which the blanks are fed by hopper. With most presses the blank is automatically placed on top of the lower die and is held in position by a restraining collar, which will be plain or milled depending on the type of edge required. The upper die is then squeezed down onto the blank with a force of up to 100 or more tonnes, so that the blank receives the impression of both dies while at the same time the metal is forced outwards to take up the shape and pattern of the collar. The rate of striking depends on factors such as the size and design of the coins but with the sophisticated engineering of modern presses 400 coins can often be struck in a minute. A new generation of presses is likely to be faster still, achieving rates of up to 700 coins a minute.

After striking, the coins are automatically ejected from the press and fall into a container for inspection. A statistical

Above. A robotic arm at work stacking bags of coins.

sampling technique is used to ensure a rigorous quality control and after passing inspection the coins are counted into bags and check-weighed, the first task on which a robot has been used in the Mint. The bags are then conveyed to a secure area to await despatch, either overseas or by road to cash centres in the United Kingdom. Samples of all United Kingdom coins except bronze are taken for submission to the Trial of the Pyx which continues, as it has done for more than seven centuries, to provide an independent check on the accuracy of the coins struck by the Royal Mint.

A separate proof coin section is responsible for the special coins which are struck for sale to collectors. Since the seventeenth century proof coins have represented the perfection of the minter's art, and it is the combination of traditional skills and modern technology which has enabled Royal Mint proofs to reach their current level of excellence. The dies are given a matt finish and then a craftsman, using diamond paste, carefully polishes parts of the surface to produce a pleasing contrast between the frosted features of the design and the mirror background of the field. The blanks, too, are specially polished, either by burnishing or buffing, before being struck in a dust-free atmosphere.

Below. Polishing a proof die; and inspecting a proof coin after striking.

Right. The proof coin unit.

Proofs are struck one at a time on a coining press and receive more than one blow from the dies to ensure that every detail of the designs is faithfully reproduced. The dies are kept clean and are replaced immediately they show any sign of deterioration. After striking, each coin is carefully removed from the press to prevent damage and once it has satisfied trained inspectors it soon finds its way into the attractive packaging which is a feature of these special issues from the Mint.

Die-Making at Llantrisant

Modern die making has been transformed by the introduction of the reducing machine. The traditional method whereby engravers cut a matrix or punch by hand, a painstaking process which might easily take three or four weeks, has now been largely superseded by the machine, which produces a master punch in relief from an electrotype copy of an artist's plaster model. The first of these machines to be used in the Mint was acquired by Benedetto Pistrucci in 1819 and a second was officially ordered for William Wyon in 1824; but it was probably not until the turn of the century, when machines were purchased from Janvier of Paris, that the Mint began to make full use of the reducing machine.

The plaster model, prepared either by a private artist or by a member of the Mint's small but highly skilled Engraving Department, is usually between six and ten inches in diameter.

Right. Stages in die-making; the artist at work on his sketch; the preparation of a plaster model; the growing of the electrotype; and an engraver perfecting the steel matrix.

A silicon rubber mould is taken from the model and after one day's curing to make it pliable and flexible the mould is made electrically conductive to enable it to be plated with nickel. After about two hours it is transferred to a copper plating bath, where it is left for three days to allow a sufficiently thick deposit of copper to back up the nickel on the mould. It is this nickel-faced copper electrotype which is then mounted on the reducing machine.

The machine is essentially a three-dimensional pantograph, so simple in its operation that the Mint craftsmen are still happiest with the old Janvier machines which were transferred from Tower Hill. The details of the electrotype, set firmly in wax and revolving slowly at one end of the machine, are scanned by a tracer at the free end of a rigid bar. The movements of the tracer as it follows the contours of the electrotype are communicated by the bar in reduced amplitude to a rotating cutter at the other end. The cutter, as it moves in and out, accordingly reproduces the details of the design at coin scale onto a block of steel to form a master punch with features in relief as on a coin. A first, or rough, cut takes a day, to be followed by a second cut which takes another day.

Minute blemishes and flaws are removed from the reduction punch by hand. It is then hardened so that it can be placed in a hydraulic press and its design transferred under pressure to a piece of soft steel. On this new tool, called a matrix, the design is incuse and it is at this stage that the engraver is able to add by hand the beads, the figures of the date or any other feature not included on the original model. Once work on the matrix has been completed, it is hardened and then placed in a hydraulic press to produce the working punch. This, like the reduction punch, is in relief, and after turning and shaping it is returned to the engravers for final adjustment and cleaning. It is from this punch that working dies, all absolutely identical, are made for the coining presses.

Above. An engraver ensures that there are no flaws or blemishes on the matrix.

Right. One of the Janvier reducing machines at work.

To protect their surface and prolong their life the dies are chrome plated. Even so the life of an individual die remains a little unpredictable, though most now comfortably exceed 200,000 coins.

The Modern Royal Mint

Above. The new twenty pence and one pound coins.

Today the Royal Mint has become both a business and a Government Department. Since 1975 it has operated as a Government Trading Fund, giving it a degree of commercial freedom but at the same time requiring that income should not only balance expenditure but that there should be an additional return on the capital employed. The Deputy Master, who remains a civil servant like the 1000 or so other members of the staff, presides over a board of directors and acts as chief executive. After ten years under the new system, cumulative sales have exceeded £600 million and the Mint has operated profitably in each of the ten years, achieving an average return on capital which compares favourably with the private sector.

Acting under contract with the Treasury, the Mint continues to be responsible for the production and issue of the United Kingdom coinage. In recent years it has had to cope with the introduction of two new coins, the 20 pence and the pound; the ½ penny, on the other hand, has been demonetised and withdrawn, and the Mint is constantly exploring with the help of outside experts the ways in which the coinage might develop in future. Commemorative coins have become rather more frequent, with particularly successful crown pieces being issued in 1977 for the Queen's Silver Jubilee and in 1981 for the wedding of HRH The Prince of Wales. In 1986 a special two-pound piece is being issued for the Commonwealth Games, the first time that a sporting occasion has been commemorated on the United Kingdom coinage. All new designs continue to be submitted to the Royal Mint Advisory Committee which, under the Presidency of HRH The Prince Philip since 1952, now normally meets at Buckingham Palace.

Above. Silver Jubilee commemorative crown, 1977.

The striking of overseas coins has remained a large and successful feature of Mint output, reflecting a deservedly high reputation for quality and delivery in a business which has become more and more competitive. In most years well over half of total production is exported and in the financial year 1984/85, for instance, the Mint struck coins for no fewer than 67 countries, ranging from Ascension Island to Zambia. Sales staff based in the London office make regular trips overseas, and the Mint co-operates in a consortium with two private mints in Birmingham and the Currency Division of the De La Rue Company to ensure that as many orders as possible are won for the United Kingdom. As part of its service to overseas customers, the Mint also operates with De La Rue a joint company, Royal Mint Services Limited, to provide advice and technical assistance to foreign mints. Results have been such that since the Mint moved to Llantrisant it has twice won the Queen's Award for Export Achievement, first in 1973 and then again in 1977.

Above. Commonwealth Games two pounds, 1986.

United Kingdom proof coins. *Right*, gold proof coins of 1985 and *below*, base metal proof set, 1986.

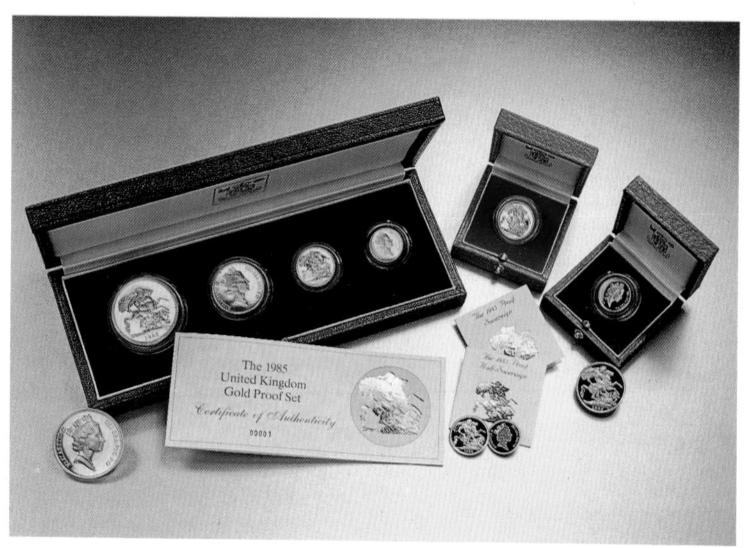

Above. Five pounds of 1984, struck in brillant uncirculated quality.

An increasingly important aspect of Mint activity has been the sale of proof and uncirculated coins to collectors. Following the outstanding success of the sets of the last £sd coins of 1970 and of the first decimal coins of 1971, proof sets of United Kingdom coins have been struck every year. An expanding range of proof and uncirculated United Kingdom and overseas coins, in gold and silver as well as base metal, is now available by direct mail order from Llantrisant. The regular issue of colourful Bulletins and brochures has been a new departure and the Mint has become a frequent exhibitor at shows and conventions, particularly in North America, which has proved a highly receptive market for collectors' coins.

Below. Silver medal given to Mint staff to commemorate the winning of the Queen's Award for Export Achievement in 1973.

Right. Privy Seal of the Duke of Cornwall. (Actual size 73.5mm)